THE AMERICAN POETRY REVIEW/HONICKMAN FIRST BOOK PRIZE

The Honickman Foundation is dedicated to the support of projects that promote spiritual growth and creativity, education and social change. At the heart of the mission of the Honickman Foundation is the belief that creativity enriches contemporary society because the arts are powerful tools for enlightenment, equity and empowerment, and must be encouraged to effect social change as well as personal growth. A current focus is on the particular power of photography and poetry to reflect and interpret reality, and, hence, to illuminate all that is true.

The annual American Poetry Review/Honickman First Book Prize offers publication of a book of poems, a $3,000 award, and distribution by Copper Canyon Press through Consortium. Each year a distinguished poet is chosen to judge the prize and write an introduction to the winning book. The purpose of the prize is to encourage excellence in poetry, and to provide a wide readership for a deserving first book of poems. *House and Fire* is the sixteenth book in the series.

House and Fire

For Courtney + Travis —
TA

House
and Fire

MARIA HUMMEL

American Poetry Review

Philadelphia

Cover art: *Rift 11*, Carol MacDonald
Book design and composition: VJB/Scribe
Distribution by Copper Canyon Press/Consortium

Library of Congress Control Number:
ISBN 978-0-97189-812-7 (pbk., alk. paper)

9 8 7 6 5 4 3 2 FIRST EDITION

For Kyle, Bowie, and Bruce

ACKNOWLEDGMENTS

A huge thank you to all the editors of the journals in which these poems first appeared:

32 Poems: "The Unicorn"; *America:* "Quiet Hours"; *Bellevue Literary Review:* "Strawberries"; *Born* Magazine: "Solstice"; *Crab Orchard Review:* "Glass After Glass," published as "Sans Merci"; *Crazyhorse:* "Sleep Barnacle," "Puzzle," "Carousel, Ten Days After His Third Transfusion"; *Diagram:* "Dear Sirs"; *Four Way Review:* "The Angels"; *The Missouri Review:* "What to Say," "Changeling," "714B," "Twelve Red Seeds," "White Houses"; *Narrative:* "Key"; *New England Review:* "The First Turn Might Be the Right One Home"; *Pleiades:* "Ode On Sleep"; *PN Review:* "Cold War"; *Poetry:* "One Life"; and "Station"; *Post Road:* "New York Selves: An Elegy"; *Third Coast:* "Ghost Traffic."

My gratitude goes to my earliest teachers: first, my loving parents and brothers; then Robert Brown, David Huddle, Margaret Edwards, Gladys LaFlamme Colburn, Fred Chappell, and Stuart Dischell. Thanks also to Jenn Habel, my longtime friend and reader.

I could not have written these poems without the warm community of the Stanford Creative Writing Program, my generous and brilliant professors Ken Fields, W.S. Di Piero, and especially Eavan Boland; as well as so many inspiring Stegner poets, including Kirsten Lee Andersen, Greg Wrenn, Robin Ekiss, and John Evans. To the Mission Pie Poetry Society — Keith Ekiss, Sara Michas-Martin, Rita Mae Reese, and Alexandra Teague — thank you. Your guidance and your own beautiful manuscripts showed me how to make a book.

I would also like to thank the Vermont Studio Center and the Dorothy Sargent Rosenberg Memorial Fund for generously supporting me and other poets in their work.

To my son's medical team and the nurses at UCSF, most especially Dr. Emily Perito: Thank you for your countless hours and devotion to Bowie's case.

Fanny Howe, thank you humbly and deeply for this "gate as a gift." Many thanks also to Elizabeth Scanlon, *The American Poetry Review*, the Honickman Foundation, and Copper Canyon Press.

Lastly, thank you, Bowie — your strength and radiance illuminate every page of this. Thank you, Bruce, for being born and growing every day. Thank you, Kyle, the champion of Fort Awesome, and my true love.

Contents

Introduction

"O my comforter in sorrow, my heart is faint within me."

These words from the prophet Jeremiah resonate around this collection of poems, where poetry *is* the comforter during a terrible time. When I read the manuscript, I did not know the poet, her name, or even what happened. All I knew was that her relationship to words was rooted in necessity and drew me back to the Orphic origins of poetry for the first time in a while.

Poems are not prayers and they are not greater than paintings or songs, they are not aimed at a known audience, but they are usually lonely laments and protests or testaments and sometimes ecstatic avowals of existence. Sometimes they overlap with psalms and tracts but they are not expected to exceed subjectivity with more dark presence. Opening is the goal, the balance between in and out.

> Who wants to open a world
> in on itself: the sweat, the brick, the body,
> the same white bed empty
> and filling, empty and filling?

In this book of poems, the medium is the messenger. Poetry brings comfort to the poet, and thankfully she knows it, uses it, she has practiced for years, you can tell. Each poem brings stern requirements too, along with its interests in coincidence and signs, its order and timing, its certainty that it will all come together. The work is exerted on the poems so the poet can endure a prolonged hardship; it is a record of sanity sustained by practice.

A child is very ill; there is a hospital. There are other people. There is a house and a tree. These are not nursery rhymes or cribs and crayons, but they have the feel of these, of all that we have in common with everyone else who was and is a child. The subject is as basic as a bowl and a nail, wood and a house and a house on fire.

> For every crooked bone
> there's a straight bone, for every face, another face;
> and in this suffering place we now call home
> is a boy who walks and plays while he lies alone.

If the practice of poetry is a kind of yoga, then this book proves it. Without the poet having put the long work on language and sound behind her, she would have lost her balance and we would have lost the consolation of this collection.

Fanny Howe

House and Fire

Station

Days you are sick, we get dressed slow,
find our hats, and ride the train.
We pass a junkyard and the bay,
then a dark tunnel, then a dark tunnel.

You lose your hat. I find it. The train
sighs open at Burlingame,
past dark tons of scrap and water.
I carry you down the black steps.

Burlingame is the size of joy:
a race past bakeries, gold rings
in open black cases. I don't care
who sees my crooked smile

or what erases it, past the bakery,
when you tire. We ride the blades again
beside the crooked bay. You smile.
I hold you like a hole holds light.

We wear our hats and ride the knives.
They cannot fix you. They try and try.
Tunnel! Into the dark open we go.
Days you are sick, we get dressed slow.

Daughter
Granddaughter
wife etc
Grandson ...

3

Cold War

I had three brothers to watch over me.
I had a collie, a yard with lilies-of-the-valley.
I had a father, mother, birthdays, ice cream.
At two, I played at drowning. At ten, I dreamed
of nuclear death, and whenever a plane went
coasting over, it marked the end. A cloud bent
back on itself. Our house and all its hills
peeled and boiled dry — neighbors spilled
out like rice into the rubble and bone-dust
of my mind's eye. What kind of child entrusts
herself to suffering, vowing *I alone will live*
to the autumn corn answering *live,*
live on, along the red rivers and farms?
Like a bride I waited, touching my inner arms.

Changeling

Sweeping into the house
after hours away from you,
I am certain they have come:
moss-footed, quick as a root,

their black hands lifting,
their red hands taking,
their white hands
setting this sleeping body

in your place. I carry you
like the hill carries its trees,
all over nowhere, until you
are mine again, swollen

with the hindmilk of evening.
Only then do I enter the
kitchen, and slice mushrooms
for supper, the ones I waited

too long in line to buy. I
barely have to press the knife.
They smell like damp hair.
They wrinkle and shine

in the frying pan. When was
the last time I heard you cry?

Ode on Sleep

In grief and motherhood

    it comes like rain too late to save the fields

in childhood
      like moon-vine   in adolescence

        a mayonnaise   too thick for the mouth

   in old age   the last love kiss

              so deep

      a mineshaft could not reach it

    even the one I am already building

            for the day

      you leave me

down there   where rock breaks to water
              everything shakes

     whales the color of coins long buried

    rise from the clay   singing

            dreams of the afterlife

chosen, chosen

rough beams

splintering   like the ship

that once carried

hollow statues   shirts from China

and a kind man who let the small fish go

Dream visions .

Ghost Traffic

All night   they blow by   the sleek fat cars
from the decade of my birth   with its war
and bad gas mileage   death of the elm
low as boats   they have nowhere to go
but back and forth   they lay patches
roll down windows   to let out smoke
motown's slow-blue   *baby, baby, don't*

leave me   like the wagons   jogging
west on iron springs   and the hopes
of immigrants   to own a scrap of
bottomland   soft enough   for the hand
to sink to the wrist   or the revs of
motorcars   the laughter   and violet
sashes   of ladies   who drove them
who are gone   into the bright   silent
headlights of time   as the Novas
and Darts are going   will go when I

think of my death   I think of grief
loss   a contingency   not this
drone   of ghost traffic   backed
up for ages   so busy   lonely
I almost lose   the man in the Cadillac
chewing stale gum   humming to himself
one of the new songs   about wanting
wanting what you can't have   wanting
so bad   his arm hooked over
the empty seat beside him   where
there's room enough   for this whole
city   or just someone   pretty and
missing   as a precious daughter

714B

We are finally quiet now,
my baby son beside me,
the machines slipping their spit
into his veins.

Rain splashes the window.
The doctors flash and vanish.
His crib foams over with toys.
He has nowhere else to play
and I take them out when he sleeps.

I hear a distant moan,
the nurses' feet
rushing, then stuttering
before they reach a door.

Who wants to open a world
in on itself: the sweat, the brick, the body,
the same white bed empty
and filling, empty and filling?

I don't envy the nurses their jobs;
they avert their faces from mine:

smiling at this small limp boy,
lifting a rattle for him,
setting it down,
turning the pages of a book for him,
saying *where's the baby? show me the baby.*

The Unicorn

A father crashed into the ward one day, carrying it. The creature was big enough to stagger him, but delicate, too, like a robe of white velvet. A long gash pulsed at its throat — red soaked the man's hands and wrists — but the unicorn was still alive. Every few seconds, its legs shuddered and its head lifted, in a movement so musical it reminded me of waterfalls. The horn scraped the paint on the wall.

The father kept adjusting his grip, passing his son's room, then ours, all the way to the nurse's station. Each day the doctors in the hall talked longer about his boy's regimen. Just this morning, I heard the word *lost*.

In the father's face, pain was surfacing too fast, like the skinned trees that sled on a spring-swollen river.

The animal in his arms fought to breathe. Its white fur glistened.

"You got a pot big enough to cook this down?" the father shouted at the nurses. "We need to make some medicine."

Altar

Here are the cups we drank from.

Here are the stones we chinked
together to make a hearth,
the scar of blue embers inside.

Long ago, we stood in this place,
opening our chests
to the flames and smoke.

And you took my heart.

I took yours,
a weightless lump of char
between my ribs and spine,

so I could live
with your lightness for years.

Quiet Hours

How can I get used to this
half-lit room, the tubes, the saw-like cry
of another mother's child? The kiss

of silence, later, when nurses listen,
then drop their eyes, sleep upright.
How can I get used to this?

I don't miss my innocence
but wish I could remember when I
was my mother's child, kissed

tear by tear, back to happiness.
Red bags fill him a seventh time.
How did we get used to this?

I have another, uglier wish:
To rip out all the needles, the wires.
He'd be my child again for an instant.

The hall lights dim. A mother makes lists
as her baby screams. A mother lies
awake, weeping, because she is used to it.
A mother gives her child a kiss.

Rounds

Each day we all come out to meet Dr. B
with a feast and singing,
puddings, pills, verse, refrain,
sheets stained
with need and wine. The nights
grow cold
from the ground up
under the shadow of his towers.

Whenever dark falls,
one of us winds her fingers over his arm,
thin as ribbons,
her pretty face leaning in,
unwilling to say it,
Will my baby live? If I just knew
he would live.

Go on and eat now,
he tells her,
save your strength.

And under her eyelids
the ocean strains.

Under her feet, the bent floors
straighten.

Carousel, Ten Days After His Third Transfusion

I watch the horse
our son is riding
glide into gallop. Forward,

around: the proud, cratered
nose, serrated mane,
coat like black water.

Up! Down! our son calls, giddy —
holding the stake
driven through its body.

Ultrasound

When you were born, which you are not yet,
and grew up, which you have not done,
loved another, which you have not found,
and lasted long in life, which you may,

I gave you this: somewhere there is a tree
that grows its leaves on the inside.
Somewhere a forest that rustles and hushes
in no breeze. Where stones float
and rivers sink below them. Where wine
climbs the throat in white vines,
and the wind is not a whisper
or song or sigh, but the rising
of the ink inside your eyes.

And there, where nothing stays long,
death will be the pressure of a seed
into the earth, and the seed a boat.

When it's time, step into it.
Let it take you back to this dark
apse, the soft folds swaying.

I will be waiting all around you.

Puzzle

The trains stall, blue and green,
beside a circus, a carousel.
Every day there are missing pieces

and I find them under the sheets,
your metal bed.
                    If you get well
we'll build a train, blue or green,

and ride it to the rocky sea,
jump waves, and grab for shells.
I miss every day.
                    Piece by piece,

I set the sky. You make the scene:
ponies leaping up poles, a girl
in blue beside the tall green train.

The empty box waits. It deepens
as our fingers slow, cannot fill
the day. The missing pieces

erase the rails, strip the shade tree,
break the face of the girl.
Every day there are missing pieces.
The trains fall, blue and green.

There Is a Story

There is a story about a mother who never gave birth.

She lived in a mountain village. She grew her child like any other wife. She swept her stoop, full-bellied. The gauze of sunlight bound her face. A snowpack seized the skyline all winter, and gave way with the thaw-winds and the sounds of owls mating in the woods. The village swelled with babies, but not hers.

For that first year, her neighbors found her rounded figure beautiful. Then they pitied her. They forgot to notice her straining back, her swollen breasts. Her house grew neglected. Her husband left town.

When she died as an old woman, the child finally slipped out. Some said it was not a baby at all, but a thick late frost that killed the crops. Some said it was a ray of the moon, balled and white.

Although they kept silent, every mother knew better.

What to Say

I'm sorry is the first wrong thing.
My thoughts/prayers are with you.
I know a family with a child like yours, a story about the girl they bore.
She's still alive, past sixty, past the time her parents could care for her.
She's in a home, and here's the bittersweet:
She loves it, thinks it's school.
All her life she had to watch her siblings go.
Now she's ready to learn alone.

The day your news came, I went to an exhibition
on the city's worst quake. On display: someone's mosaic
of family photos — yard poses, fishing trips,
and two ruined houses at center, rafters barbing the sky.
I did not think of you, but I wondered
when that artist knew
the separation between expectation and hope.

I want to say: Thank you for your letter.
I don't know how hard this is. If today the weight of holding him
is more than yesterday. I don't know what I would do,

but I heard of a family like you:
They have a son. They set him in his crib.
They spread a blanket over him.
Together they whisper a song they fear he won't understand for years.
A shaky music fills the room — a rising scale,
the sliding foundations of sleep.

Later, when his needy cry wakes his mother,
she stumbles up, she unbuttons, she lets him lock to her.

Her milk spills down
his throat, the sound
louder than a wet eye blinking, but quieter,
so much quieter
than the traffic going by all night.

The Tree

which was

in equal parts
earth and sky

is now in equal parts

house and fire

At Night, Late, Tar Pit

When the man presses
the frame of the woman, she opens, a door
to thick black water. This is the west;
distances are deep. Or maybe there's more
to the scene: their baby in the next room
is coughing and neither one can sleep,
and the clothes they tossed to the gloom,
unwashed, start making oily love, heaped
in the carpet. Or maybe the dark beneath
the bed and crib is reaching for itself.
Whatever is clutching, growing, heaves
its way up like spring. It soaks the shelves
and blankets, the bodies, and sinks them one
by one for six thousand years, until dawn.

Strawberries

Today your arm eats strawberries.
Tomorrow, birthday cake and toast.
The tubes go in, their liquid clear.

As our life at home grows far
and faint, food becomes a ghost.
Today your arm ate strawberries.

I read you books on dinosaurs,
their lost hungers, fallen bones.
The tubes go in, their liquid clear.

I once loved words, their
fat red flesh, their roar and moan.
Today your arm eats strawberries

and what it tastes can never
be named or held or known.
The tubes go in, thin and clear,

sewing your skin to poles and air.
I once loved a meadow,
its clear little stream, lying there
on my arms, eating strawberries.

I stack myself like construction paper

color of sorrow and color
of relief

      color of hospital curtains on chains

         of puzzles trains staircase hillside goats winterless
                                   California

lone tree

        lone tree

ultrasound static

hundreds of gray leaves
twitching around you

and my first thought:

how safe

resolve

said Dr. Lee

your body is resolving

they could remove you or I could wait

for thirty-three years

I didn't make anything

with my body

                  and then
your brother

                  and then
he sickened

watching him sleep
              hooked to tubes

an empty envelope
inside me

fills each dawn
with one long love letter

by night
           it's mostly apology

in the waiting room

they call
Maria

I and a lumbering lady
in her eighth month

both rise

in the waiting room
                              the full Maria
passes me at the door

cupping
herself

the way water
cups a hull

        that day they take you
out

      I hear

         the silence
of the lake

that never
drowned me

though for years
               I watched it

       over the rails
of ships

beyond the window-frame

whitecaps

swaying

your unmaking:

drain-language

slurry

while a man says clearly
        and far away

a little pain now

                        (in every movie
                        about love

                        blood appears

                                though sometimes
                        it disguises

                                        its face

                        as a red dress
                        autumn

                                        strawberries
                        wetting a plate

wind
        drifts
                the city park shines

                    its undersides

your brother four years old
home again

grabs the grass
tugs up

grunting *I'm trying to lift*

the earth

            I take my place
      beside him

                blades bend

as I tighten

my fists

the ache for days

will remind me of

will remind me

Solstice

Someone is turning the light
down on the world

moths go mad
with the lack

of desire

people forget to waken

but all it takes
is somewhere

a yellow field

a girl chucking
stones at a nest
of wasps

and the black alphabet
unscrolls

from its paper sheath

writes across her face
and hands

all the pain
for which time is

meaningless:

the wings
a passing train
parts from the body

she calls love

the rainthirst
under the eyelids

she calls leaving

and when they are done

the sting
enters the sun

the faint day

begins to taste again
like honey

but the sad thing

the girl will be
convinced

for a long time

she was extraordinary
to survive that
afternoon

with a perfect
abiding

fear of bees

that she will owe
each of her lovers

o tender secret

she whispers
to their sweat-glazed bellies

and pale inner wrists
all the soft

exposed places

Glass After Glass

It was wine in the mouth, a house
with silk pillows, a man at the piano,
and, turning fourteen, my tight braces
making my conversations ache — when
the Italian woman (who was invited,
no, not invited, but came, wearing her
dark rope of hair and pouring glass
after glass of sour cabernet) said to me
You're so beautiful and meant it, like she
had just claimed a view about to be
eclipsed by clouds, and my own loud
face stared back, burning to hear those
words again and never again, on the lips
of men and women. How different it was
with women, who surprised themselves
by saying it, and often turned away.

Yet the fool I was, I believed this
made me a stranger among the rest,
repeating *beautiful* against my cool
sheets, and *beautiful* as I entered the din
of school. It would be years before
a boy said it, bending to block the light.
I would kiss the possession in his voice
to hear it echo in my mind. *Beautiful.*

The Italian woman must be old by now,
and I am her age. I taste the same wine
as I watch the faces of girls, but it is
sweeter than I thought, this grief
over fading, the way we wish just one

evening would outlast us with its tender
intensity, would go on staying red
and gold, while we change and change.

New York Selves: An Elegy

1.

My favorite one: I die dramatically on the streets and end up in the memory of a future filmmaker. He gives me red mittens, snow, a lover who said something he regretted, a train speeding over tracks.

This is the I-am-too-late-for-my-life self.

An interlude of needy piano music, cherries in a small white dish in the kitchen. My movie lover swallows them whole, one by one, having heard there is poison in the pits.

2.

Dumb dog with rich owner.

I pretend to be interested in love when I am only interested in food.

I walk the springy mud of the park, sniff poops leftover from January icebergs, go home, get washed long and golden.

If the earth could breathe, I would be its third or fourth song.

3.

I should leave out the bohemian self the one always drinking

white tea/wine with a dozen friends who live in the cruddy

apartments history awards geniuses shuffling from one party

to another smoking lovemaking regretting waking and doing it all

over again this is the self my mother drove from me with every

atom of love in her bones beat me black and blue with pride

don't be one of those people who won't grow up those selfish selves

(but someday I run into hers climbing from a first-floor window

satin shirt hanging off her shoulders and a man's voice inside

calling her back Sweetie I didn't mean it Crazy girl as her blond

hair falls in front of her face like milk running down the wall)

4.
Tonight the knight
will try and fail to pick up
a dozen girls, their mouths
closing out his kisses,
and I will be the one
who gives in, finds a tower,
a witch, a spell to help
him feel the hero.
I'll even throw in a free
ambiguous ending
in case he falls in love
with me: an accident
outside his window
in the empty morning.
Two red cars crippled
around each other,
and both drivers screaming
how could you not see me?

5.

The one who runs away

always runs to California.

Becomes a gorgeous postcard

scrawled with blue ink.

What season is it?

I wonder if you can grow old

if you don't know the years

are passing. And to me,

the self that stayed, too

safe to reinvent, a patriot

of fixed rent and thin pizza,

these questions always

seem less than they are,

like the palms on the reverse,

not trees exactly, but someone's

neat drawing of trees, someone

who hasn't learned perspective.

Dear Sirs

Thank you for sending me my invisible robot arm.

For all those wires and guarantees, I expected it
to throw and lift, at least to punch,
but it doesn't.
          It only holds.

It started with a glass, then a sponge, a table, a room,
a skyscraper, an iceberg.
          It thinks it can keep the world together
by grasping.

Right now it has seized you and me, and we don't even feel it.

We don't know what it's like to be alone
when we're solitary in the car, strolling with our tan coats
pulled close against the wind, watching the news
explain again
          the way wars go.
It has a slow deep way of pulling us closer.

But you promised me mighty, elbow, flex, and fists.
Where can I get with this?

Where can I walk on this whole earth
without carrying everywhere and everything I've been?

Twelve Red Seeds

Twelve red stains
on the sidewalk. Twelve suns
at the edge of a picture,
each colored the wrong bright shade.

Something will come to lick them up:
the earthworm dying on its way
to the garden, a sluggish
skunk, the soapy brush of a mother

who does not want her son to ask
whose or why. Briefly, she wonders
if the blood is hers.
She has a hole in her side

she probes when no one is looking
to feel if it still pains her. It does. It will
not heal. It will not kill her.
Her boy is beautiful and ill.

She can no longer see the days
when she washed his body
and thought it perfect, gossamer,
blue-threaded,

his small fist closing
around the root of her finger
in an unbreakable ring.
Yet she wants to teach him

so many things: Look at these Os
blurred to blots, these tears
of the sad, red giant!
Look at these stars, starry nights, star pins, star fish.

Cole's Pacific Electric Buffet

California, a pair of boots for the summer.
California, a summer of pairs, this fruit,

that falling house by the sea. This cook
fighting with that Saturday over

who invented the French dip. Juice
dripping from the chins of the market,

sawdust clinging to a boot. The man
slicing my sandwich points to the body

of my line, his knife sweeping breast
to thigh, and he smiles. Lust for the lost

tooth is a black gap between cars
at night, and I am horny in another

parking lot. Saturdays drift like
sawdust, intentions falter. I dream

of every night the sea. It suspends
its body over me, California.

I taste the man who dipped me once,
halfway back to an invisible bed.

I taste the cook who humped
the hot space between his waist

and the summer on that last day
of fire, who turned away from

my blush, grinning and tonguing
the dark between his teeth, red beef

shoving through boots of bread,
his crude and delicious invention.

Immunology

In the blood's deep, the monsters
came shaped like flayed octopi, mined
their way through tissue. It wasn't enough

to kill them. It wasn't enough
to call more guards. To defeat such monsters
the body needed memory. The first mind

was this mind: it recognized *mine*
from *other* and declared war. Enough
millennia gone, and memory is the monster

now — a tentacled, many-Septembered wine,
I want to find you here: black hair, buffed
yellow car, cassette-tape dancer —

but my monstrous mind isn't enough.

The Angels

They have not come for you. They will not blister
the day with light and swords. The room remains
a room, and not a portal. The syringes
hold no messages, not even plain
emptiness. The food trays, when you eat food,
rattle if I move them, and, if left alone,
sink beneath an ice of grease. The good
doctor is pregnant, and strokes her own
belly when she speaks. In a thousand years
no one will remember any of this.
The hospital will be a ruin. Your
tubes twisted in a dump, or burned. But if wrists
are stumps, hands are trees: I lift yours to learn
how the wind moves. Hold them to know where it turns.

One Life

I don't know when I stopped believing in heaven,
or if I do. Maybe I just stopped receiving heaven.

A winter day: I climbed into the pines' brittle
crowns. You could say I was retrieving heaven.

Not a place or a time, but blindness to all
but one light, pulsing, pleasing: heaven.

We married in September. Everyone was still
wearing their summer shirts, sleeves of heaven.

It was white, there was a bend, and the car
spun. It was then I prayed, pleading with heaven.

When he goes limp, lie him down on the gurney,
Mom. Oxygen mask, breathing heaven.

The hospital shines, our son flies in and out.
The snow falls hard, relieving heaven.

He loves the colors of planets. I teach him
their lifelessness: beautiful, deceiving heaven.

I don't know who is buried beneath me,
but I hear her break as I am leaving heaven.

How can you cry for one ruined life, Maria,
when you could be grieving for heaven?

A Thousand Faces

In the creation myths of pumpkin,
bellies grew first, billowing out
before the light, the sea and flowers.

And the bellies commanded the void:
let there be hollows in this darkness
and arches hung with pulp as soft

as the inside of a cheek; let there
be a cathedral for seeds, a favorite
purse in the garden's green closet.

So the pumpkins grew into portly
multitudes that try not to trumpet
their superiority, each laden

with irreplaceable burdens,
each shape original and derivative,
the plump bulge of matrons,

taut barrels of elderly generals —
and what of that color? Is there
a wish in this world that can blush

as beautifully as the pumpkin?
Gold for secrecy, red for richness
and blessing, a yam paint

mixed with the flush on a girl's
face the first night she realizes
how to possess her body, then

darkened by rain, autumn, waiting.
The love affairs of pumpkins
are always long, full of slow kisses

and vacations postponed
in favor of staying on the mound,
savoring some peace and quiet

for once, this fragile forever.
In the lame stories of pumpkin
heroes, the bravest line up at dawn

to be carved and shattered for the glory
of harvest, but the waning garden
refuses to cheer for them, or perhaps —

like the sea and its waves, or a mother
watching her sons ride away — it merely
calls too softly for them to hear:

Come back, let me open
for you again, you are mine,
you would never break inside me.

Children's Ward

for Damien

I.

In the bed beside yours, the child is so small
he could fit in a lady's purse, a shoebox.
He smiles but doesn't say anything at all.

You fall in love with him, wake up calling
Baby! Baby! pull our curtain back, knock
the reeds of his crib. The child is so small

he barely sees you, or the picture on the wall
you drew for him, of rain and broken robots.
He smiles but doesn't say anything at all.

He's one year old, cannot roll or crawl,
and floats alone all day while we play and talk.
The room around us is so small.

When his mother comes, she is beautiful,
her dark hair a sail, her face made of knots.
She smiles but doesn't say anything at all

as we sit, holding our sons until they fall
asleep. Then she goes, the room closing like water
after a passing boat. The child is so small.

He smiles and says nothing at all.

II.

The tiny boy has a twin brother at home.
"Nothing the matter with him," his mother says.
The brother walks and plays. This boy lies alone.

You are our only child. Yet somehow I know
what she means, what I almost pray:
you, too, have a twin, a brother at home

who never hurts, was not broken,
pierced by wires and bandaged again.
That boy walks and plays. He stays alone

while we live here. He grows cold
in those empty rooms, as the daylight fades.
I'm afraid he's dying. But if we get home

he'll be waiting in the dent on your pillow.
He'll whisper in your ear, shake you awake
until you walk and play. It's a lie we come alone

into this world. For every crooked bone
there's a straight bone; for every face, another face;
and in this suffering place we now call home
is a boy who walks and plays while he lies alone.

Sleep Barnacle

Because it happens after I turn out the light,
sink into the hull, after the night-weeds grow
over my eyes, because I go to bed alone
and troubled, because I can't remember when
you were well, or what a day
was like without you, because in a place

where there is no way out, our place
is *within*: each night, an unseen light
slices into your room, and, unlike the day,
it wakes you crying, until you grow
out of your bed and down the hall, and when
you climb up into mine, we are still alone

but one creature. The dark, too, is alone
and with us. It is a place
like water. It is the hour of blackout when
people can't find candles to light
so they sit down and listen. My hair grows
into your fingers; your belly is a day

blooming from my spine. A day's
ride inside its hollows, a hundred lone
craters wait. Red berries grow
all over them; inside each is a place
that looks like a temple when light
falls through it, and sounds like a howl when

breath reaches it, and when
the berries ripen, throughout that day,

heavy birds with lightless
eyes arrive, seeking to eat. You won't go alone
if you go. Each of my dreams is a place
that begins in your hands, that grows

into your body, beating, as flesh grows
into a voice that goes on singing when
the singer has lost her throat. A place
as gray as grief survives as a giant rainy day
in memory. My lonely
son or my drowning, I see a ship of light

or the sea; I see you alone one day
growing older, growing the places you'll know
or the light, and when it goes, I'll go down.

The First Turn Might Be the Right One Home

On a strange road, the first turn you see
might be the right one home,
as at a party, the first man you meet
might be the one worth noticing.
That is, if you're lost looking
for a man, or a road, don't let your hands tighten
and move too soon. Turn even once,
you can't go back: Think about the first time
you were ever asked to dance.
Then think about the last.
The first turn in a pool is to the deep
end. The first turn to religion is,
like the first kiss, most uncertain and holiest;
the first house you own with someone else
is loneliest at night when he is gone.
The man and you make
a child, and it changes you together,
as when a sunstruck window
sways all the plants in a room
the same direction toward the light.
Clocks turn to tell time, so you believe
the hours *pass by* instead of spinning you
inside them. Day turns to night
like paper to a love letter, until the ink
spills all across the sky. The child
turns a lamp on and off, *on! off!*
he delights in power, and does not see
how it will alter him. To *turn into* is
to become; *turn up*, to arrive; *turn away*,
to go deliberately blind — but you don't

turn older. You grow its complexion:
you can't remember another Italy
than the one you visited at twenty,
or how you used to pray. The child turns
the faucet on and lets the silver
rush his palm. His father is turning
pages in a magazine, and looking up from time to time
to see the bath swell and deepen. Years ago,
he turned to watch you walk in your cotton dress.
The water brims. The naked child
turns pink, then fish inside it. Your wishes
have become so simple
and tender: *Let us have this love.*
A ring is made of turns, but you can't take them.
You only let them grip a single finger.

I'm This Many

Are monsters real or not? Is God? Why do
needles hurt people's arms? I don't think
I understand *everything* yet. Red drinks
taste good with straws. When I'm asleep, do
you see my dreams? How did Dinosaur
Land become People Land? Are my legs
longer today? Do stars grow from eggs?
Can I eat like other kids when I turn four?

How many weekends to my birthday?
I want a round cake. I want your hair.
I think the medicine I take for snakes-
in-my-stomach is making me cough.
Can you put me to bed now? The air
is dark outside tonight. Who turned it off?

Unbinding

Die Entbindung (German): childbirth, release

Now, in my last month,

      time begins to spin, as summer spins
against the cool hands of the field,
and yields its sleeping places
under roots and pond mud
to the creatures who need burial
to live.
      I alternate basking
and frantic preparation.

Even water tastes like ripe fruit,

and I am so thirsty and
so full. Yet I already know

what to keep:
just one memory, or two,
of holding
this new life inside.

      In the first,
I step into the sea; it lifts me
to a hull, barely
anchored by my toes.

      In the next, I step into the
sea. It covers me; all I see

is blue-green, green-brown,
gold falling slow as hair
or snow, or snow.

Fog

Here it comes with the color of sleep.
The city slips into its gloves, sleeps.

The gray seas shove onto the damp
beach, the way dreams shove sleep.

Your birth: I will be a white fortress,
red gates, rising from plains of sleep.

The summer circles us like wet cloth,
blinds. I reach for fire, touch sleep.

Not this time. Not this child. An-
other room, other bed, another sleep.

I hear the whistles, but I never see
trains arrive, not at night, not asleep.

These clouds of salt: they make roofs
over my life, where blue doves sleep.

How does the daughter become the mother?
Under the white moon, above sleep?

Oh, Maria. You've always loved
morning light because you love sleep.

White Houses

Once you understand the lost situation of the leaf
dragged on a slow stream, snagged by roots unhooking
from the bank, and that the limit to the sky is a rough
red earth and the limit to earth is its own rising;

once you understand the lifting wind lifts
the thorns easier than the fruit, fells the fruit
to the dark sob of ground beyond the reach of bird
or hand; once you build your white house on

the highest hill, only to find this makes it closer
to storms and the ghosts of others who failed this land;
once you understand why the glass breaks in the dishpan,
shaving a flap of skin above your thumb, so the suds

bloom red as trillium in a forest where no one has been;
once you stop looking for ways the glass should not
break, thorns should not prick, the house not shudder
against the wind — then the bright shards will fall

like rain on the parched riverbed, then the black
thread will stitch your skin back to rags stretched
over a loom of bones, and when the yard blooms its flat
offering of violet and clover, you can cut them down

without fearing they're your own heart shorn to the root;
you can wander out on the battered streets at night,
alone as a god, listening to the stopped hiss of hydrants
and alleys choked with weeds, missing who you were

when you believed in a world of consequence and
white houses, when you needed to be told you mattered.

Key

this comb   for the ghost's hair
this ridgeline treeless and sheer

it smells like tea   gone cold
weighs less than a vein pumped full

it rolls the stone away from the cave
at dawn   rolls it back at night

and one day   it falls into
the snow   grows into a slender

black tree   to shelter your way
though for a long time   you

walk right through it   live
your life   as if dread has not

changed you   lock the house
from the inside   shut

the drapes   huddle before
the little door   in the hidden wall

behind which   the child
rides away   on a flat white bed

About the Author

Maria Hummel's poetry and prose have appeared in *Poetry, New England Review, Narrative, Creative Nonfiction,* and *The Open Door: 100 Poems, 100 Years of* Poetry Magazine. She is also the author of two novels: *Motherland* (Counterpoint, 2014) and *Wilderness Run* (St. Martin's, 2003). A former Wallace Stegner Fellow, she teaches at Stanford University and lives in San Francisco with her husband and two sons.